Acting Cool!

Using Reader's Theatre to Teach Math and Science in Your Classroom

By Chris Gustafson

LINWORTH
LEARNING

From the Minds of Teachers

Linworth Publishing, Inc.
Worthington, Ohio

Copyright © 2003 by Linworth Publishing, Inc.

Library of Congress Cataloging-in-Publication Data

Gustafson, Chris, 1950-
    Reader's theater : science & math / by Chris Gustafson.
        p. cm.
    Includes bibliographical references.
    ISBN 1-58683-151-8 (pbk.)
    1. Drama in education. 2. Readers' theater. I. Title.
    PN3171.G89 2004
    371.39'9--dc21

                                          2003012886

Editor: Claire Morris
Design and Production: Good Neighbor Press, Inc., Grand Junction, Colorado 81503

Published by Linworth Publishing, Inc.
480 East Wilson Bridge Road, Suite L
Worthington, Ohio 43085

ISBN: 1-58683-151-8

5 4 3 2 1

Table of Contents

Table of Contents *(continued)*

Science

National Science Education Standards • 57

 How to Use This Book

Reader's Theatre is a wonderful tool across the curriculum. Although specific topics taught at each grade level vary nationwide, national standards that promote excellence in most content areas do exist. Seeing a connection between national standards and a particular teaching unit is sometimes difficult. The plays in this book reinforce national standards by using situations that reflect best teaching practices and are fun for students. They are intended for use by middle school students, though some may be appropriate for lower or higher grades as well.

Each play comes with vocabulary, before reading, and after reading activities, many with grading standards. Use your own creativity and knowledge of your class either to alter, omit, or add to these activities.

A bit of extra time will be needed the first time you use a play. Begin by asking if any students know what Reader's Theatre is. Only a couple of my students had any idea what was involved at the beginning of the year, so be sure students understand that Reader's Theatre is like doing a very short play, but no parts are memorized. Go over the following expectations for the performers:

- Skim over your parts to make sure you can pronounce all the words. Ask for help if there are words you don't know.

- Speak loudly enough so that you can be heard at the back of the classroom.

- Communicate using expressive voices and faces. Sound effects are encouraged, too.

- When you are not reading, do not draw attention to yourself by your facial expressions, fidgeting, or making noises.

The grading standard on page 1 is intended to help evaluate a Reader's Theatre performance, and can be filled out by the teacher, the student, or both. It's also effective to have a class imagine the best possible Reader's Theatre performance, and use their ideas to create their own grading standard. Evaluating the performance of the audience is easy. The job of the audience is to listen attentively during the performance and clap politely after it is done.

Even if you don't use the vocabulary activities, there are probably some words in the piece that not everyone will know. They are listed before each script in this book. Depending on the reading level of the students you are working with, you may need to talk about what the words mean and how to pronounce them. You can add words, omit words, or skip this pre-teaching altogether, depending on your class.

There is a list of the characters before each script, with brief character descriptions. These should help students convey their characters since they won't have had time for more than a brief look at their part. After you've described the parts, ask for volunteers, but make it clear that you will assign parts if necessary.

If you are using a script that introduces a piece of literature or a historical character, it's helpful to give a brief introduction to the time period, the setting, and possibly the characters in the book. Some ideas for this summary are included before each literature script. A good time to do this is after you've handed out the scripts and while the actors are glancing over their parts, which will be highlighted on each of the separate scripts, to make sure they can understand the words they're going to read

When it is time for the play to begin, students stand in a line facing the audience. Ask them to say their character's name before they begin reading the script. This helps the audience to remember which student is reading the part of which character. It also helps the actors get a sense of how loudly they will have to read to be heard. It's an easy time to ask individuals to read more loudly. You can ask the actors to group themselves in a way that shows how their characters are related to each other. When they're ready, the reading begins.

Reader's Theatre works with regular education students, highly capable students, English language learners, fluent readers, average readers, and even those for whom reading is challenging. The occasional group comes in thinking they are "too cool" to perform; but once they have done it, most are anxious to do it again. ***Enjoy using these plays with your class!***

Name _____ Period _____ Date _____

Grading Standard for Performance

1. I used my voice and my facial expressions to make my reading interesting.

1	**2**	**3**	**4**	**5**
boring				lively and interesting!

2. I stood quietly when it wasn't my turn to read.

1	**2**	**3**	**4**	**5**
bothered my neighbor				stood quietly

3. I read clearly and fluently.

1	**2**	**3**	**4**	**5**
forgot what quite a few words sound like				read clearly

4. My voice could be heard by the people in the back of the room.

1	**2**	**3**	**4**	**5**
they fell asleep from boredom				they heard me

5. I did my best and I'm proud of my performance.

1	**2**	**3**	**4**	**5**
blew it off				made myself proud

Total points _____

 # Math Content Areas

The following content areas are incorporated into the *National Council of Teachers of Mathematics* curriculum standards, Principles and Standards for School Mathematics.

Data Analysis

Probability

Geometry

Measurement

Number Sense

Algebra

Skate or Swing? Let the Data Speak

by Chris Gustafson
NCTM 1, Data Analysis

Vocabulary Activity

Give each team of students a copy of the *Skate or Swing? Let the Data Speak* Vocabulary page. Ask students to cut apart the boxes, sort them into three or four groups, and give each group a title. Students explain to the rest of the class the reasons why they grouped their words as they did.

Vocabulary Words

agenda—plan or schedule, often for a meeting

data—objective information

graph—a diagram representing mathematical relationships

improving—getting better

investigate—to explore, look into

lopsided—a bit tippy

pathetic—truly sad and woeful, worthy of pity

PowerPoint®—a computer program used to produce slides for an oral presentation

sample group—a small group that shares the same make up as a larger group

scanned—converted from graphic or text to a computer file

skateboard—board on wheels

slumped—bent over

superficial—on the surface, not important

survey—a set of questions

topic—a particular focus of interest

Before Reading

Divide students into groups and give each group a recent local newspaper. Give each group ten minutes to locate and list all the ways they see statistics, graphs, or other forms of numerical data in the paper. Have groups report their findings. Encourage students to see the practical use of these math tools.

Perform *Skate or Swing? Let the Data Speak*

Cast of Characters

> *Narrator 1*
> *Narrator 2*
> *Mr. Lee—pushes folks to do their best*
> *Aisha—bored*
> *Jerome—aspiring class clown*
> *Pedro—organized*

After Reading

Ask students to brainstorm current issues in their school—the dress code, sale of junk food, etc. Individually, in pairs, or as a group, have students choose a position on their issue. Then have them describe three ways they could use numerical data to support their position in a letter to the principal, school board, or other decision-making body. Work with students to create a grading standard to evaluate their letters.

Skate or Swing? Let the Data Speak Vocabulary

agenda	investigate	sample group	superficial
data	lopsided	scanned	survey
graph	pathetic	skateboard	topic
improving	PowerPoint®	slumped	

8

Skate or Swing? Let the Data Speak

by Chris Gustafson
NCTM 1, Data Analysis

Narrator 1: The data collection/graphing project sheets were passed out.

Narrator 2: The groups were assigned.

Mr. Lee: All right, people! You have five minutes to brainstorm survey questions for your graphing project. You'll need to collect a lot of data. Be sure to pick a topic everyone can get excited about.

Narrator 1: Aisha, Jerome, and Pedro pulled their chairs closer together.

Narrator 2: Pedro pulled out a piece of paper.

Pedro: I'll write down our ideas.

Jerome: Favorite sports! Everyone has an opinion about that.

Narrator 1: Aisha yawned.

Aisha: Yeah, right.

Pedro: Aisha, don't you have a favorite sport?

Narrator 2: Aisha didn't smile. She stared at Pedro.

Aisha: That's such a boring question. How could you ask anybody that without cracking up?

Jerome: Okay, I guess not. How about favorite movies?

Pedro: Or how often people go to the movies?

Jerome: Or video games? Or lunch room food?

Pedro: Too easy. The data would be too lopsided.

Mr. Lee: Don't be superficial, people. Tackle tough questions. Investigate something that matters. Look for big issues. Collecting data is a way to do important work.

Narrator 1: Pedro looked down at his list.

Narrator 2: Jerome grabbed it and read it over.

Jerome: No big issues here.

Pedro: How about grading policies? Too much homework? Those are big issues. Or I could just write bigger.

Narrator 1: Aisha slumped down in her chair.

Mr. Lee: Two more minutes.

Jerome: Come on, Aisha. You're not helping.

Pedro: Yeah, if our ideas are so stupid, what do you want to do?

Aisha: A skateboard park.

Jerome: What?

Aisha: My Mom's on this neighborhood committee. They want to take that corner by our school playfield that belongs to the park department and put in some play structure for little kids.

Pedro: By those pathetic swings?

Aisha: They want to spend all this money to make it a great place for three-year-olds. It's not fair! It's right by our school! Why don't they make a skateboard park instead?

Jerome: Well, did you ask your Mom? What did she say?

Aisha: She said she never thought of that. I guess all the rest of the people on the committee have little kids, and they figure they'll be three years old forever.

Pedro: That's it! We'll show them the park shouldn't be just for little kids! We'll design a survey. We'll need a big sample group and really good questions.

Jerome: Then we'll put it all together on PowerPoint®. Can you talk to your Mom, Aisha, and get us on the agenda for the next committee meeting?

Narrator 2: Aisha sat up straighter in her chair.

Aisha: I guess so. Do you really think it would work?

Mr. Lee: Time's up, people. Read over the ideas you brainstormed and put a star next to the one for your group's project.

Narrator 1: The math class met in the library the next day to plan their surveys.

Narrator 2: Pedro took over the keyboard while Aisha and Jerome pulled up chairs next to him.

Pedro: Okay, what do we need to ask?

Jerome: How many people skateboard now?

Aisha: Where do they skateboard now?

Jerome: Would they use a skateboard park close to school?

Pedro: How often would they use it?

Narrator 1: Mr. Lee looked at their computer screen.

Mr. Lee: Good job. Your group is tackling an interesting question. What are you going to do with your data?

Aisha: My Mom's on that committee about improving the park right next to the school field. They want it to be just for kids but we don't think that's fair.

Mr. Lee: What do you want them to do?

Pedro: Make a place for us, too! We think there should be a skateboard park.

Mr. Lee: Your data will help show there's a need. Try to imagine you're one of the adults on that committee. What else will they want to know?

Narrator 2: Aisha, Pedro, and Jerome shrugged.

Mr. Lee: How about how much your idea would cost?

Jerome: Oh, yeah. Would it be safe, and how to keep the little kids from getting skated on. I'll do the research on that.

Narrator 1: Jerome located a free computer and opened up his favorite search engine.

Narrator 2: Getting the data wasn't always easy.

Jerome: I can't believe it! Ms. Finch lost our stack of surveys between her mailbox and her classroom!

Narrator 1: Compiling the data wasn't always easy.

Aisha: Don't touch that! I already recorded the papers in that folder! Don't mix them up!

Narrator 2: Organizing the data wasn't always easy.

Pedro: This line graph looks so cool!

Jerome: It's stupid! You don't put data from a yes/no question on a line graph. They'll think we're idiots.

Narrator 1: There were technical difficulties.

Aisha: Where's the third slide? Did it just fall out of the stack?

Pedro: Here it is.

Aisha: No! Everything I had in black is yellow! I can't read it!

Narrator 2: Finally their presentation was ready.

Mr. Lee: All right! You're on . . . you've done a great job. Just show them that data!

Narrator 1: Pedro stood in front of the playground committee.

Pedro: Thank you for allowing us to share our data collection and graphing project with you.

Jerome: We hope you will listen to what we have to say about adding to your project to improve the neighborhood park.

Narrator 2: Pedro clicked open the first slide. It was a photo of Aisha when she was little, sitting on a swing.

Narrator 1: The second slide was Aisha's scanned-in school picture from this year.

Aisha: My Mom would tell you it seems like yesterday when I was the little girl on the swing. But little kids grow up, and that's why . . .

Narrator 2: Aisha, Jerome, and Pedro could see that the audience was paying attention. They grinned at each other and put their math project to work.

Is Everyone a Winner?

by Chris Gustafson
NCTM 2, Probability

Vocabulary Activity

Assign vocabulary words to pairs or groups of students. Give them three minutes to come up with a definition for their assigned word. Have groups report. If groups with the same word suggest different definitions, discuss and come to some agreed-upon meaning.

Vocabulary Words

blur—lose focus

data—collected information

freeloader—someone who lets others to do most of the work

probability—the chance that something will happen

rigged—designed to give a certain result

spectacular—highly impressive

Before Reading

Individually, in groups, or as a class, have students complete the first two sections of a KWL chart about probability. Since this age group is likely to answer the question, "What do you want to know?" with a resounding "Nothing," try using the phrase "What do you wonder?" for the middle part of the chart.

Perform *Is Everyone a Winner?*

Cast of Characters

> Narrator 1
> Narrator 2
> Narrator 3
> Latisha—kind, outgoing
> Katie—confident, a little judgmental
> Ms. Yamagata—stern, keeps things moving

After Reading

Have students fill in the final column of the KWL chart. This play might suggest more things students wonder about, and they could be added to the middle column. If students aren't very clear about how probability works, they may not be quite sure Kirk and Josiah ran into problems with their game. Have students complete the problem/solution statements on the problem/solution sheet.

Name _____ Period _____ Date _____

KWL/Probability

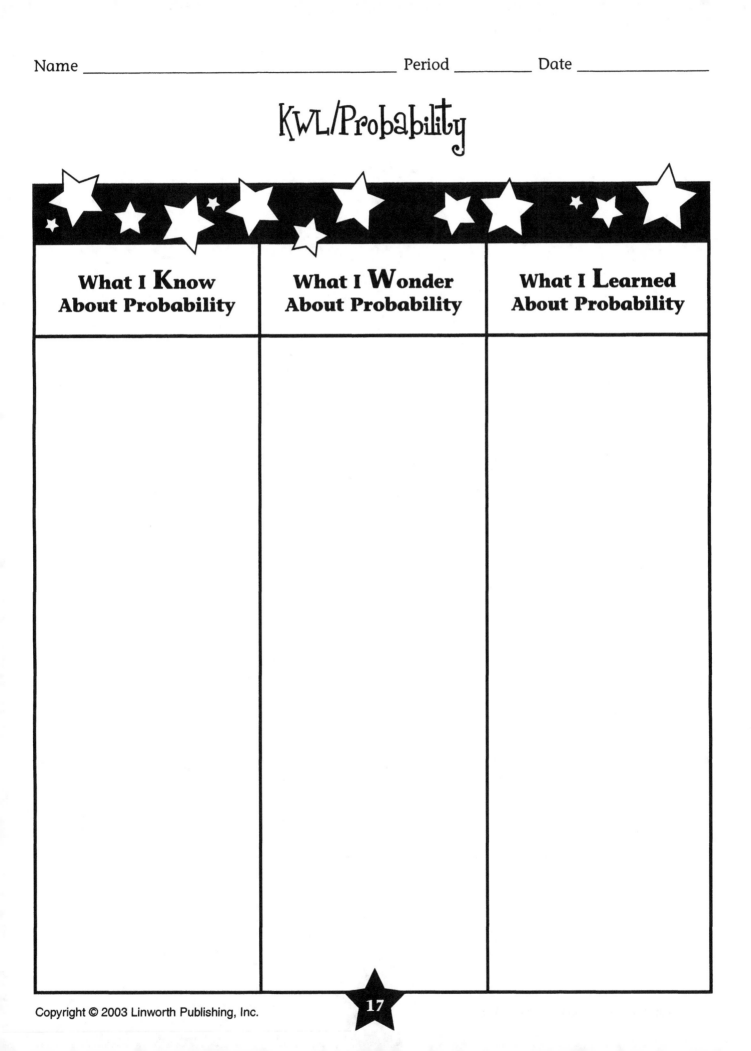

What I **Know** About Probability	What I **Wonder** About Probability	What I **Learned** About Probability

Is Everyone a Winner?

by Chris Gustafson
NCTM 2, Probability

Narrator 1: The poster outside the lunchroom door read "Welcome to the Probability Fair."

Narrator 2: Inside, five math classes were putting together their probability games. Each team of students had four feet of table space to decorate.

Narrator 3: Latisha twisted purple and gold crepe paper and taped it along the front of their table section, while Katie propped up their sign. It read "Spin to Win" in huge, glittery letters.

Latisha: I've got the Kit Kat® bars in my backpack. Do you think we should have made a prize box?

Katie: Leave them there until someone wins. I don't want you-know-who to grab one.

Narrator 1: Katie glared at the next table space. It was empty except for a sloppily lettered sign that read "Kirk and Josiah's Awesome Bag of Chance."

Latisha: Josiah's not so bad. I wouldn't care if he won our game. Maybe he'd share his Kit Kat with me.

Katie: I don't get why he teamed up with Kirk. Kirk was on my team last year when we did our "Create a Country" project. Kirk created absolutely nothing! He is such a freeloader! And a candy grabber.

Narrator 2: Katie and Latisha carefully arranged their wheel of chance on their table space.

Narrator 3: It looked spectacular! They had made it in wood shop; and they were especially proud of the way the spinner turned smoothly over the level board.

Narrator 1: The sections of the board were brightly painted. Katie twirled the spinner.

Katie: Look how level it is! Ms. Yamagata can't say our wheel is rigged because it's uneven. Do you have the data collection sheets?

Latisha: Right here.

Narrator 2: Ms. Yamagata blew a whistle to get everyone's attention.

Ms. Yamagata: Ten minutes until we start. One partner will remain with the game and record data while the other partner goes out and plays games. After half an hour I'll blow the whistle and the partners will switch jobs.

Latisha: You go play the other games first.

Katie: Okay. Look, there's Kirk and Josiah.

Latisha: Finally!

Narrator 3: Kirk dropped a plastic grocery bag onto his table space. It landed with a slight clicking sound. Josiah spilled his grocery bag out on the table. Fun size packets of M&Ms® tumbled out.

Narrator 1: Katie whispered to Latisha.

Katie: Do you think they bothered to read the grading standard for this project? You know, the part that says the game has to be well made and show a lot of effort?

Narrator 2: Ms. Yamagata blew her whistle.

Ms. Yamagata: Let the games begin!

Narrator 3: The next half hour was a blur for Katie. She recorded the results of every spin, and barely had time to look up between players.

Katie: Next.

Latisha: It's me. How are we doing?

Katie: Great! Did you win a lot of candy?

Latisha: Some. I mean, did we design the game right? Remember what the project sheet said about winners?

Katie: Carnival games are always designed so the people playing them lose more often than they win. We don't get full points if we have too many winners.

Narrator 1: Katie glanced at the data sheet.

Katie: It's fine. Just enough people are winning. We did a super job!

Narrator 2: A whistle cut through the lunch room noise.

Ms. Yamagata: Switch! Partners switch.

Latisha: Go on and play, Katie. Be sure to try Yuko's game. I think she messed up on the probability part; but it's an easy place to win some licorice.

Narrator 3: Finally the crowd around "Spin to Win" thinned out a bit, and Latisha had time to check out Kirk and Josiah's "Awesome Bag of Chance" just as Ms. Yamagata showed up at their table.

Ms. Yamagata: Not much of a line here, Josiah.

Narrator 1: She read aloud the directions printed on a piece of notebook paper next to the grocery bag.

Ms. Yamagata: Draw a green M&M and you win. Plus you get to eat the M&M.

Narrator 2: Josiah held up the bag and Ms. Yamagata poked her hand in and drew out an M&M. It was red.

Ms. Yamagata: Let me see your data sheet.

Narrator 3: As she looked at it, Josiah stared down at the table.

Ms. Yamagata: Any idea why you only have one winner when your data shows that forty people have played?

Narrator 2: Josiah looked into the grocery bag. Then he emptied it out on the table.

Narrator 3: Two red, three blue, one tan and one brown M&M fell out.

Ms. Yamagata: After you had a winner, did you replace the green M&M?

Narrator 1: Latisha had to cover her mouth to keep from giggling.

Narrator 2: Josiah's mouth twisted down, and Latisha felt sorry for him.

Latisha: It must have happened while Kirk was running your game. Don't feel bad.

Narrator 3: The whistle blew for the final time.

Narrator 1: Katie arrived, breathless.

Katie: Latisha, how'd we do? You were right about the licorice. I won tons!

Narrator 2: Latisha didn't hear Katie. She was busy breaking a Kit Kat bar in half with Josiah.

Is Everyone a Winner? Problems and Solutions

In the *Is Everyone a Winner?* Reader's Theatre, find the problems to the solutions that are listed. Then imagine what might happen to Latisha, Katie, Kirk, and Josiah during the rest of the Probability Fair. Write two problems they might face, and a possible solution for each of those problems.

1. **Problem:** _____

   Solution: Latisha kept the Kit Kat bars in her backpack.

2. **Problem:** _____

   Solution: Katie and Latisha took turns playing other people's games.

3. **Problem:** _____

   Solution: Ms. Yamagata poured the M&M's out of the bag.

4. **Problem:** _____

   Solution: Katie shared her Kit Kat with Josiah.

Imagine what might happen to Latisha, Katie, Kirk, and Josiah during the rest of the Probability Fair.

5. **Problem:** _____

   Solution: _____

6. **Problem:** _____

   Solution: _____

This Isn't Math, It's Art!

by Chris Gustafson
NCTM 3, Geometry

Vocabulary Activity

Make enough copies of the vocabulary word page so that when they are cut apart there is one word for each student. Pass out or have students draw a word, then use the word in a sentence that shows the meaning of the word. Give a short time for this activity; encourage use of a dictionary or the internet. Group students who have the same words and have them share sentences with each other, choose one sentence to read to the whole class. Briefly introduce Paul Klee, an artist who used geometry in his paintings.

Vocabulary Words

artistic impression—how good something looks

Cubism—a school of painting featuring geometric shapes

Fibonacci Series—a set of numbers, each the sum of the two previous numbers, which demonstrates a pattern often found in natural objects

newsprint—very thin, oatmeal colored paper

Paul Klee (pronounced Clay)—an artist who used geometry in his paintings

rhombus—a type of parallelogram

sketch—a preliminary drawing

spiral—a coiled shape

technical merit—judging based on required elements

vivid—brightly colored

Before Reading

Pass out the anticipation guide. Give students a few minutes to agree or disagree with each statement.

Perform *This Isn't Math, It's Art!*

Cast of Characters

> *Narrator 1*
> *Narrator 2*
> *Jake—goes with the program*
> *Cameron—frustrated, a little stubborn*
> *Mr. Ochoa—encouraging, not easily rattled*

After Reading

Give students a few minutes to revise their anticipation guides and write briefly why they changed their answers. Have students discuss in small groups how they responded to each statement, why they responded that way, and why they may have changed their answers.

After studying geometric shapes, show students work by painters who clearly incorporated geometry into their work, such as Picasso, Paul Klee, Mondrian, and Jacob Lawrence. Work with students to create a grading standard for a painting that would demonstrate an understanding of a number of geometric shapes. Have students create a painting and evaluate their work. Put on a Gallery Walk!

Name _____ Period _____ Date _____

This Isn't Math, It's Art! Vocabulary Words

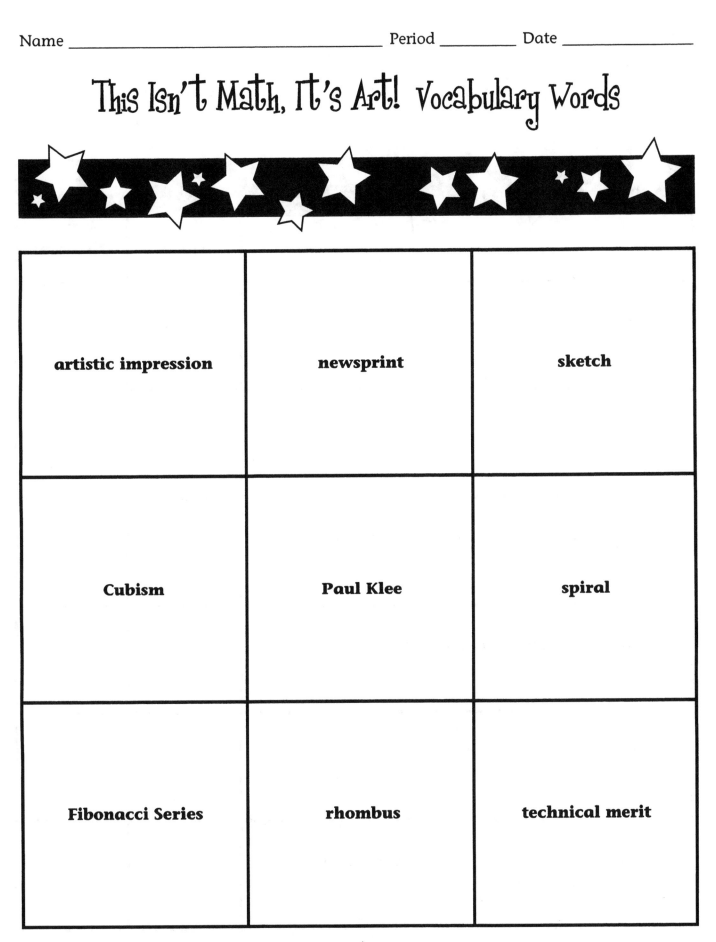

artistic impression	**newsprint**	**sketch**
Cubism	**Paul Klee**	**spiral**
Fibonacci Series	**rhombus**	**technical merit**

This Isn't Math, It's Art! Anticipation Guide

	Agree	Disagree
1. People who are good at math aren't good at art.		
2. Artists use geometry in their work.		
3. There's more to math than solving problems.		
4. Art projects shouldn't be graded.		
5. It's good to integrate what you learn in one subject with what you learn in another subject.		
6. You could show what you know about geometry by making a painting.		

28

This Isn't Math, It's Art!

by Chris Gustafson
NCTM 3, Geometry

Narrator 1: Jake and Cameron bent over big pieces of newsprint spread out on tables in the library.

Cameron: This is not math. I am good at math. This is art. I stink at art.

Jake: Be quiet. Stop complaining.

Cameron: Why do we have to do this? Just give me a page of problems.

Narrator 2: Mr. Ochoa, their math teacher, stopped by their table.

Mr. Ochoa: Your draft is looking good Jake. You'll be able to start your final piece tomorrow.

Cameron: Mr. Ochoa, I used to have an A in math. Please, please give us a test for our geometry final. Don't make us paint a geometry picture! I'll flunk and then I won't get into a good college and my parents will kill me.

Narrator 1: Mr. Ochoa looked hard at Cameron's sketch. He sighed.

Mr. Ochoa: Fortunately, this project will not be judged like ice skating. Your grade depends much more on technical merit than artistic impression. Just include the required elements and you'll be fine.

Cameron: So I get a decent grade because my painting has the right number of shapes and angles. But everyone will laugh at it on the night of the gallery walk.

Narrator 1: Jake looked at Cameron's sketch.

Narrator 2: He laughed.

Cameron: Even my best friend thinks it's stupid.

Narrator 1: Jake pointed to the top of Cameron's sketch.

Narrator 2: The required shapes were drawn all the same size across the top of the paper. The rest was blank.

Jake: Uh, maybe it will look better when you actually paint it. Color helps.

Cameron: Are you trying to be nice?

Jake: Didn't you stay awake when that art professor came and showed slides of all those geometric artists? You know, those cubism guys.

Cameron: How was that supposed to help?

Jake: All those painters knew geometry . . . Paul Klee, Picasso, and Jacob Lawrence. They put shapes and color together to make something amazing.

Cameron: Paul Klee, is he the guy who painted those melting clocks?

Jake: Uh, no.

Cameron: Just give me numbers.

Narrator 1: Cameron began to write numbers next to everything he'd sketched on his draft.

Cameron: Four squares, seven rectangles . . .

Narrator 2: The next day Jake transferred his sketch to thick, creamy paper. He began to plan his colors—vivid and bright in some spots, and mixed together to make softer tints for other parts of the painting.

Cameron: Mr. Ochoa, can I start on my painting too?

Narrator 1: Mr. Ochoa looked at Cameron's painting.

Narrator 2: He sighed.

Mr. Ochoa: All right. But you need to fill the whole piece of paper. Right now, this looks like a wallpaper border.

Narrator 1: Jake worked hard on his painting.

Narrator 2: He came in during lunch to be sure it would be done in time for the gallery walk.

Narrator 1: The night of the gallery walk, the school lobby was brightly lit.

Narrator 2: All paintings were mounted on exhibit boards that looked like room dividers.

Mr. Ochoa: Welcome, Jake! Welcome, Cameron! Grab some cheese and crackers and look around.

Narrator 1: Jake and Cameron had seen all the paintings in class. Now they looked different mounted on the exhibit boards.

Narrator 2: Each painting had a neatly typed title, the name of the artist, and a short essay explaining how geometry was used.

Jake: Look at Lizzy's. She really did paint the Titanic going down.

Cameron: Especially if you stand back and squint a bit.

Jake: Pablo did his whole painting in shades of green.

Narrator 1: Cameron looked at it critically.

Cameron: Artistic impression is fine. But technical merit? I don't see the required rhombus!

Narrator 2: Jake stopped in front of his own painting. He grinned.

Cameron: "Landscape," by Jake Washington.

Jake: It's just how I wanted it to look.

Narrator 1: Mr. Ochoa came by and handed Jake and Cameron each a filled cup.

Mr. Ochoa: Have some apple juice guys. Jake, what do you think?

Cameron: Jake's trees look like they're going to fall over.

Jake: It's cubism, you jerk.

Mr. Ochoa: Good job, Jake. If the ice skating judges were rating your painting, you'd do just fine in both categories.

Mr. Ochoa: Now Cameron, let's take a look at your entry.

Narrator 2: Cameron led Mr. Ochoa and Jake over to his painting.

Mr. Ochoa: Wow! What happened to the wallpaper border?

Cameron: I knew it was stupid. That's why I did this. Do you get it?

Narrator 1: Mr. Ochoa looked carefully at the painting. It looked like a huge spiral, filled with different shapes and colors. Mr. Ochoa grinned.

Mr. Ochoa: All right! It's the Fibonacci Series!

Jake: It is?

Cameron: I used the proportions to make the spiral. Then I made the number of shapes to match the series.

Jake: One circle, one rhombus, two triangles, three squares . . . it's all there.

Mr. Ochoa: Well done! Full points!

Cameron: Jake, don't you dare laugh!

Jake: Not me. You can hang this in your dorm room in that good college. Super job.

Social Life in a Box

by Chris Gustafson
NCTM 4, Measurement

Vocabulary Activity

Divide students into groups. Assign a word to each group, and give them a few minutes to agree on a definition for each word. Report back.

Vocabulary Words

advertising—promoting a product

concave—hollowed out like the inside of a bowl

container—an object made to hold things

mascara—eye make-up

net—what you get when you cut open a 3-D shape and flatten it out

overlap—one edge flaps over the other

rectangular—Shaped like a rectangle: a geometric shape with two sets of parallel sides and four right angles

UPC code—product bar code

Before Reading

Make an overhead and use as a class, or give copies of "Jobs Using Measurement" to students in groups. Collect ideas of jobs that use measurement inside the circle. Put the sources of those ideas (reading, personal experience, observation, etc.) outside the box.

Perform *Social Life in a Box*

Cast of Characters

Narrator 1
Narrator 2
Ms. Marquez—creative, well-organized
Deangelo—dreamy, careful
Mercedes—enthusiastic, self-absorbed

After Reading

After lessons on measurement, ask students to plan and create their own product packaging. Work with students to create a grading standard for their packaging that would clearly show how measurement was used to make the container for their product.

34

Name _____ Period _____ Date _____

Jobs Using Measurement

List ideas about what jobs use measurement inside the large circle. List the sources for your ideas outside the circle.

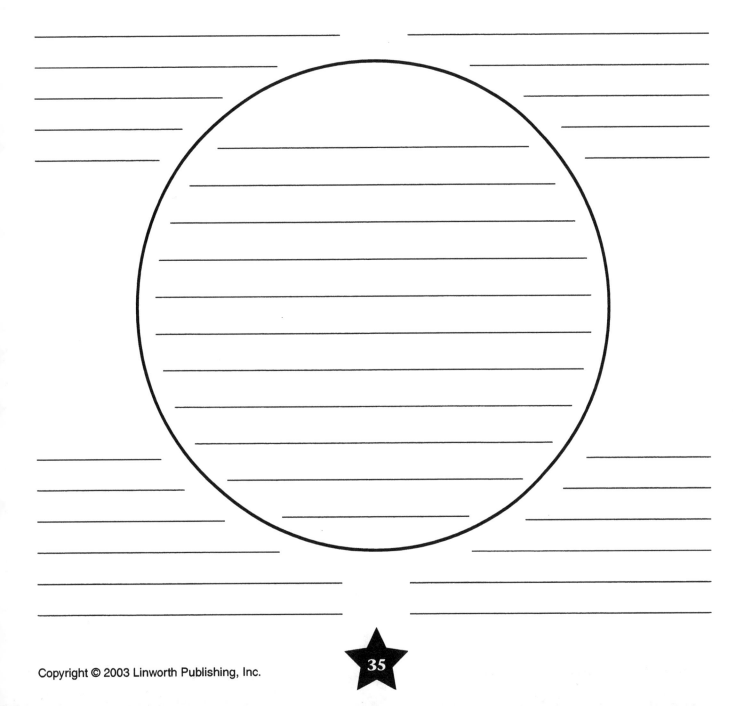

Social Life in a Box

by Chris Gustafson
NCTM 4, Measurement

Narrator 1: Ms. Marquez's math class had been studying measurement for weeks. Today they had a guest speaker to introduce their final project.

Narrator 2: Mr. Rollins ran his own package design business. He told the class how he used measurement every day in his work, and he showed samples of packaging he'd designed.

Narrator 1: Everyone liked the boxes Mr. Rollins made to ship bowls for a local potter.

Narrator 2: The soft-sided packages for candy imported from Japan were the best! Mr. Rollins put in a pull of air before he sealed them so the candies wouldn't get smushed. It didn't hurt that he passed out a bunch of the packages so everyone could have a taste.

Ms. Marquez: Thanks, Mr. Rollins, for coming to our class.

Narrator 1: There was brief, polite applause.

Ms. Marquez: Okay, everyone, I know you're wondering about the final project for this unit. Imagine that each of you has been hired by someone to create a package for a product. This happens to Mr. Rollins every day.

Deangelo: What kind of package?

Ms. Marquez: Good question. The container you make can't cover any more area than the top of your desk.

Mercedes: Do you have to have the actual product inside?

Ms. Marquez: If you can't put in the real product, put in a model of it. Don't spend more than $5.00 on this.

Narrator 1: Ms. Marquez kept on adding details. In addition to the finished package, everyone would have to turn in a net of the package shape and a chart with complete measurements of the package. The outside of the package would be just like something you'd see in the store with name, UPC code, and all.

Narrator 2: Deangelo only half listened, but he put the project assignment sheet carefully in his binder. He could check out the details later.

Mercedes: Deangelo, what are you going to make?

Deangelo: I don't know.

Mercedes: I already wrote down five ideas! A box for my own brand of cereal. Mercedes' Munchies! Or something for make-up—Mascara by Mercedes! Or . . .

Narrator 1: Deangelo stopped listening to Mercedes and tuned in to Ms. Marquez.

Ms. Marquez: Think of something you want to sell.

Narrator 2: Deangelo knew what he wanted to sell. He wanted to sell Melissa on the idea of going to the spring dance with him.

Narrator 1: Melissa was in Deangelo's gym class, and sometimes they played Ping-pong together. She was easy to talk to and easy to look at.

Narrator 2: Ms. Marquez had stopped talking. Deangelo bent over his paper and started to sketch.

Mercedes: What are you drawing, Deangelo? It looks kinda like a heart.

Deangelo: Huh? No, it's not.

Narrator 2: He erased, then sketched some more.

Narrator 1: The class worked every day on the project.

Mercedes: I thought I was going to make a really fancy shape. Like maybe a flat rectangular bottom and a concave top. But it's too hard.

Deangelo: Are you going to put mascara in that? It's pretty big.

Mercedes: No, it's not for mascara. I'm making a package for wash-in/rinse-out hair streaks. Silver, gold, and lime green all in one package! Your box is so little. What's your product?

Deangelo: I'm not sure yet.

Narrator 1: Actually, Deangelo was sure. At home he had carefully designed the faces of his small, rectangular container.

Narrator 2: He had double-checked all his measurements and charted them neatly. He hadn't forgotten to measure the overlap for the places where his box was glued together.

Narrator 1: On the day, the project was due, Deangelo carefully glued all the advertising and decoration onto each face of his small, rectangular box. It was just big enough for a card he'd made on his computer, inviting Melissa to the dance.

Ms. Marquez: Please put your container on your desk along with your grading standard. Everyone, take time to walk around and take a look at the other projects.

Mercedes: Deangelo, are there teeny roses in your box?

Deangelo: No. That's just the decoration on one side.

Mercedes: Let me see the front.

Narrator 2: Deangelo turned the box toward Mercedes.

Narrator 1: Mercedes read what was written on the front of the box in large red script.

Mercedes: "Social Life in a Box. Contents: one invitation to the spring dance." That is so cool! Who are you going to give it to?

Ms. Marquez: Deangelo, I'm ready to grade your project now.

Deangelo: Ms. Marquez, as soon as you grade it, can I take it with me?

Narrator 2: Ms. Marquez looked at the name on Deangelo's package and smiled.

Ms. Marquez: You sure can. Just leave the other pieces of the project here.

Narrator 1: The bell rang. Deangelo grabbed his package and hurried out into the hall.

Narrator 2: If he hurried, he could meet Melissa at her locker.

The Budgeting Queens Sleep Over

by Chris Gustafson
NCTM 5, Number Sense

Vocabulary Activity

As a class or in groups, have students complete the vocabulary definition page.

Vocabulary Words

budget—a plan to limit spending
dorky—not cool
freaked out—seriously upset

Before Reading

Brainstorm with students all the different ways they spend money during a month. Ask students to choose ten of the ways that were listed, and assign each budget item a realistic amount of money based on their current actual spending habits.

Perform *The Budgeting Queens Sleep Over*

Cast of Characters

Narrator 1
Narrator 2
Yumiko—organized
LaVaughn—edgier than the others
Becca—resourceful, healthy

After Reading

Have students keep track of their spending for a week, then use the data they collect to extrapolate a monthly budget. How could they use the data they collect to demonstrate to parents/guardians their responsible use of money?

Vocabulary Definitions for The Budgeting Queens Sleep Over

Define each word by finding a category the word belongs to, and listing characteristics of the word. The first one has been done as an example.

1. **Budget** is:

   • a way of planning spending that divides up a certain amount of money.

   • lists the ways money will be spent.

   • doesn't plan to overspend.

2. **Dorky** is:

   _____

   _____

   _____

   _____

   _____

3. **Freaked out** is:

   _____

   _____

   _____

   _____

   _____

43

The Budgeting Queens Sleep Over

by Chris Gustafson
NCTM 5, Number Sense

Narrator 1: Yumiko was having a sleepover.

Narrator 2: LaVaughn and Becca came over to help her plan it.

Yumiko: Okay, here's what my Mom said. She was NOT pleased when we had pizza delivered last time everyone came over.

Becca: I told you we should have taken the empty boxes out to recycling.

LaVaughn: And put the leftover pepperoni slices in the refrigerator. Leaving them out on the counter all night was not a good move.

Becca: She didn't find out about you calling Devin, did she?

Yumiko: No, no, it's just the money she was freaked about. Delivery pizza is pricey. So this time it's sleepover on a budget. We can still have fun. We just have to plan ahead.

LaVaughn: Okay, no spur of the moment stuff. What are we going to eat?

Yumiko: Pizza, of course. We can get some good frozen kind.

Narrator 1: Becca went over to Yumiko's computer and opened the web page for a local grocery store.

Becca: This is an okay brand. On sale this week, too.

LaVaughn: How many do we need?

Yumiko: I'm inviting six people; but I don't think Naomi can come.

Becca: Let's get three pizzas. Multiply by the sale price, Yumiko, and write down the total. Half a pizza each is enough.

Narrator 2: Yumiko pulled out her notebook and started to write.

Yumiko: That's really cheap. There's a lot of money left. Did I subtract right?

LaVaughn: Let me check. Yep, you did. How about pop?

Becca: And those little carrots?

Yumiko: Becca, look up the price of pop on line. We need to get some regular and some diet.

Narrator 1: Becca found the prices for pop and for a pound of carrots. Yumiko wrote it down.

LaVaughn: That's crazy! A pound of carrots? That's way too much! Who's going to eat them?

Becca: I will! And you should. I don't think I've ever seen you eat a vegetable.

LaVaughn: I knew a girl who ate too many carrots. Her skin got kind of orange and so did the white part of her eye. It was weird!

Yumiko: Won't happen to you, LaVaughn!

Becca: Why don't you ask people to bring snacks, too? I could bring cookies or chips.

Yumiko: Good idea.

LaVaughn: Let me see that list.

Narrator 2: LaVaughn pulled the list out of Yumiko's hands and studied the numbers.

LaVaughn: You've got a lot of money left over. Let's use it for something fun.

Becca: Renting videos?

Yumiko: I guess we could.

LaVaughn: What if everyone brought a video she liked? Then we could use the money that's left for . . . I don't know.

Becca: Oh, come on, LaVaughn. I can tell you've got an idea.

LaVaughn: Well, maybe we could get some of that wash-out hair
streaking in a bunch of different colors. Lime green, magenta, and a kind of
electric blue.

Yumiko: That would be awesome! We could all streak each other's hair.

Becca: Then if there's money left, we could get nail polish in the same colors to
match the streaks.

Yumiko: I don't think we can find prices for streaks and polish
on line. Let's all go to the store after school tomorrow and check prices.

Narrator 1: On the night of the sleepover, Yumiko lined up the pizzas, ready to go
into the oven. Regular and diet soda cooled in the refrigerator.

Narrator 2: Yumiko tumbled the carrots into a blue bowl. Old beach towels were
stacked in the bathroom to handle any spills from the streaking.

Narrator 1: Yumiko was just pulling out her favorite movie, Legally Clueless, when
the doorbell rang.

Becca: Am I first? Here's some oatmeal-raisin cookies. They're sort of healthy, but
really good. How do you think I'd look with magenta streaks? I want to be first
to try it. And I brought the best video ever—The Duchess Diaries.

Yumiko: Umm, it's okay. But the book was way better!

Narrator 1: LaVaughn arrived with four kinds of chips.

LaVaughn: Here's my stuff. Don't you look at me like that, Becca. I got one kind
that's baked, not fried.

Narrator 2: LaVaughn put two movies on the counter.

Becca: How come you got to bring two movies? We'll stay up
all night watching these?

LaVaughn: It's a sleepover. That's the point.

Yumiko: Sleepless in St. Paul—that's a good one. But Math, You Need It? What's that for?

LaVaughn: It's in honor of your Mom's budget. I know it sounds dorky, but it's a super video. We did the math to get everything we wanted, and now this is going to be a great party.

Becca: Really, Yumiko. Hair streaks—it's going to be the best!

Narrator 1: Yumiko grinned. The doorbell rang.

Narrator 2: All three girls ran to answer it.

Algebra Alchemy: You Can Drive My Car

by Chris Gustafson
NCTM 6, Algebra

Vocabulary Activity

List the vocabulary words and phrases on the board, divide students into groups of four, and introduce vocabulary skits. Adjust the number of words and phrases to match your class, copy as many Vocabulary Pages as you need, and hand each group the directions for the skits with their vocabulary word or phrase written in the blank spot. They will act out a short scene that shows the meaning of their vocabulary word or phrase, during which the word or phrase itself may *not* be used. Each member of the group must act and speak during the skit. At the conclusion of each skit, the class will guess which word or phrase was being depicted. It may be helpful to set a few group rules for classroom drama, for example, no physical contact between group members, don't depict scenes that violate school codes for violent or inappropriate behavior. Those people you see on the screen are acting, that's not real blood, so what you show doesn't really have to be happening.

Vocabulary Words

constant—something that stays the same

data—information gathered

demolition—to destroy

equation—two math statements connected by an equal sign

graph—a diagram showing data

horizontal axis—the line at the bottom of a graph

Medieval—a historical period from about AD 1000–1500

module—a chapter or section

set of trials—a number of experiments

variable—something that changes

Before Reading

Draw a small circle within a large circle on the board or an overhead. In the smaller center circle, write the word "algebra." Ask students to brainstorm all the words they can think of that relate to this concept. Then pass out the Taxonomy Sheet and have students transfer their revision words and phrases to the alphabetical list, along with any other ideas that come to mind as they are creating the lists.

Perform *Algebra Alchemy: You Can Drive My Car*

Cast of Characters

Narrator 1

Narrator 2

Danilo—enthusiastic, catches on quickly

Jolan—cautious, a bit puzzled

Ms. O'Brien—clear, patient, well-organized

After Reading

Create a class poster of careers using algebra. Ask each student to research a job (not teaching math!) that uses algebra and write the name of the job on the poster, along with the way algebra is used for that job.

Name _____ Period _____ Date _____

Algebra Alchemy: You Can Drive My Car Vocabulary

With your group, think of a short scene that would *show* (not tell) the meaning of the vocabulary word or phrase you've been assigned. Everyone in the group must have an acting and a speaking part. Do not touch other cast members, say aloud the word or phrase you are acting out, or violate any school rules in your skit. Use a dictionary if no one in your group knows the meaning of the word or phrase you've been assigned.

Your word or phrase is:

_____

_____

_____

_____

_____

_____

_____

_____

_____

_____

_____

_____

51

Name _____ Period _____ Date _____

Algebra Alchemy: You Can Drive My Car Taxonomy

A _____

B _____

C _____

D _____

E _____

F _____

G _____

H _____

I _____

J _____

K _____

L _____

M _____

N _____

O _____

P _____

Q _____

R _____

S _____

T _____

U _____

V _____

W _____

X _____

Y _____

Z _____

Algebra Alchemy: You Can Drive My Car

by Chris Gustafson
NCTM 6, Algebra

Danilo: This is going to be really fun!

Jolan: Yeah, but why are we doing it in math class? We're right in the middle of an algebra module.

Narrator 1: Danilo and Jolan were reading a list of directions off the overhead in their math class.

Narrator 2: At the top of the list, Danilo read:

Danilo: "You Can Drive My Car: a Math Experiment."

Ms. O'Brien: Listen up, class. There are directions on the overhead for a math experiment we're working on today. One member of your team needs to get the materials that are listed on the overhead. The other team member will pick up a data collection sheet.

Narrator 1: Jolan selected a long rectangle of plywood, some plastic bricks, a set of small weights, an open-topped plastic car, and a tape measure.

Narrator 2: He tumbled them all onto the floor next to Danilo's desk. Danilo was bent over the data collection sheet.

Danilo: I'm setting it up just like the one on the overhead.

Ms. O'Brien: Attention please, everyone. Who can tell me what a variable is?

Jolan: Something you can change when everything else stays the same.

Danilo: Like what Jolan buys for lunch. The constant is a giant cookie, the variable is oatmeal raisin or chocolate chip.

Ms. O'Brien: Exactly. Today you're going to be conducting an experiment and collecting data on the distance your car travels after it leaves the end of the ramp. You'll be changing two variables, the angle of the ramp and the weight carried by the car. Keep in mind that you'll only be changing one variable at a time. Yes, Jolan, you have a question?

Jolan: Ms. O'Brien, don't get me wrong, this looks like fun. But I sort of did the whole cars and ramps thing in pre-school. I thought we were learning algebra.

Narrator 1: Danilo hissed under his breath.

Danilo: Will you shut up?

Ms. O'Brien: Calm down, Danilo. Jolan, by the end of class, let me know if you still think we're not doing algebra.

Narrator 2: Jolan set up the ramp with just one brick flat under the end. Danilo held the car at the top of the ramp, the rear wheels even with the very edge. He let go.

Narrator 1: When the car came to a stop, Jolan carefully measured the distance between the bottom of the ramp and the front bumper of the car. He recorded the result on his data sheet.

Jolan: One brick, distance traveled.

Danilo: Let's hurry up and do all the trials. Then maybe we'll have time to try other stuff. Did you see that car show on TV last night?

Jolan: Ms. O'Brien isn't going to go for a demolition derby.

Danilo: Naw, not that, maybe we can make it look like one of those funny cars.

Jolan: No algebra yet.

Danilo: Yeah, there is.

Jolan: I don't think so. Just one number on the data collection sheet.

Danilo: Then let's get some more numbers. You'll see.

Narrator 2: Jolan and Danilo finished the set of trials with the plastic bricks. They were careful to add each brick sitting on its side, not on its edge.

Narrator 1: Then they left the ramp two bricks high and experimented with different weights in the car. Soon the data collection sheet filled with numbers.

Ms. O'Brien: Okay, you should be finishing up your experiments. Jolan, are you seeing any algebra yet?

Narrator 2: Jolan was busy taping colored pencils to the sides of his car. They looked a little like medieval lances.

Jolan: It's the Medieval Monster! No one messes with the Lances of Doom!

Ms. O'Brien: Jolan?

Jolan: Uh, no algebra yet.

Ms. O'Brien: It's time to get your data on a graph. Each team partner, take the data from one of the variables, either the weight in the car or the height of the ramp. Don't forget what you know about setting up a graph.

Danilo: Look at this—it's graphing out to a slope.

Jolan: Mine too. Oops, except for this spot.

Narrator 1: Danilo squinted at Jolan's graph.

Danilo: I think you need to fix the numbers on the horizontal axis.

Jolan: Right. Okay, I've got the slope too.

Ms. O'Brien: Eyes up here, everyone.

Narrator 2: On the overhead, Ms. O'Brien had written an equation. Jolan was puzzled.

Jolan: Now we're switching back to algebra?

Ms. O'Brien: We've been doing algebra all along. Who can tell Jolan why?

Danilo: The equation shows how they all work together. It's the distance traveled by the car and the number of bricks or the distance traveled and the weight in the car.

Ms. O'Brien: Does that make sense, Jolan?

Jolan: I guess so. Do you mean the equation is a way of writing down the data we collected and graphed?

Ms. O'Brien: Exactly. Why bother putting it into an equation?

Danilo: Because you don't have to keep doing the experiment over and over. You can predict what will happen by changing the numbers in the equation.

Narrator 1: Jolan was extremely surprised.

Jolan: Wait a minute! Do you mean that all those problem sets we've been solving mean real things?

Ms. O'Brien: Yep.

Jolan: You're kidding. They're not just a bunch of numbers?

Ms. O'Brien: Nope.

Danilo: I told you it was algebra.

Narrator 2: Jolan shook his head. Danilo heard him mutter.

Jolan: That's totally amazing.

Ms. O'Brien: Okay, take out your planners to write down tonight's homework. You'll be doing a little practice with this idea.

Narrator 1: Jolan untaped the Lances of Doom and wrote down his homework. The equations looked a little different to him than they had an hour before.

National Science Education Standards

1. Systems, order, and organization

2. Evidence, models, and explanation

3. Constance, change, and measurement

4. Evolution and Equilibrium

5. Form and function

Four Senses Plus One

by Chris Gustafson
NSES 1, Systems, Order, Organization

Vocabulary Activity

Write the vocabulary words on an overhead, board, or poster. Assign each vocabulary word or phrase to a small group of students. Give them three or four minutes to come to an agreement about what their word or phrase means. Have groups report back to the class and record their definition next to their word.

Vocabulary Words

description—a statement describing something

elements—parts of a whole

experiment—an operation carried out to test a hypothesis

invisible—can't be seen

liquid—freely flowing substance

matter—what physical objects are made of

melting point—the temperature at which a solid becomes a liquid

observation—looking carefully and systematically

solid—a substance that does not flow

substance—a physical material

Before Reading

Ask students to brainstorm the elements of a good description and create a grading standard from their suggestions. Have students choose an object—that they own, from the classroom, or you might create a collection of small objects and have students draw one out of a bag—then write a description of their object using four senses of their choice. Evaluate with the grading standard.

59

Perform *Four Senses Plus One*

Cast of Characters

> *Narrator 1*
> *Narrator 2*
> *Ms. Woo—earnest, a bit sharp*
> *Hunter—bored*
> *Milad—testy, goofy*
> *Magda—on task, conscientious*

After Reading

Make the "mystery substance" by pouring a box of cornstarch into a bowl, adding water, and stirring until you get a gloppy, shiny looking substance mixture. Use food coloring if you like. Give groups of students each some of this substance and let them experiment, after first setting some parameters for keeping things neat and clean. Have students write their observations of the substance.

Education Development Center, Inc. *Changes of State: An Elementary Insights Hands-On Inquiry Science Curriculum*, 1994.

Four Senses Plus One

by Chris Gustafson
NSES 1, Systems, Order, Organization

Narrator 1: Ms. Woo stood by the overhead, an overhead pen in her hand.

Narrator 2: The side of her hand was streaked blue from rubbing over the letters she had written.

Ms. Woo: Three states of matter. What are they?

Narrator 1: Hunter raised his hand, but when Ms. Woo called on him, he sounded bored.

Hunter: Solid, liquid, gas. Ms. Woo, we studied this in fourth grade.

Ms. Woo: You studied writing sentences in fourth grade too, but that doesn't mean you learned everything you need to know about them then.

Narrator 2: Hunter rolled his eyes.

Ms. Woo: Okay, everyone make your own chart and take notes. We'll be adding to this list for the next few weeks. Two categories: what you know, and what you want to know.

Milad: Ms. Woo, what if I don't want to know anything?

Narrator 1: Ms. Woo grinned at Milad.

Ms. Woo: In your case, Milad, your second column says "What I wonder." You may not want to know anything, but I know you've got questions about most everything.

Magda: I know that most stuff changes from solid to liquid if it gets hot enough.

Hunter: I know that gas is usually invisible.

Magda: I used to make Popsicles with Coke when I was little, and I always wondered why it was so much harder the time I froze diet Coke by mistake.

Narrator 2: Ms. Woo wrote down all their ideas on the overhead.

Milad: I wonder why 5th period classes always smell so bad.

Hunter: What are you talking about?

Milad: You know, right after lunch.

Narrator 1: Ms. Woo wrote down Milad's question in the second column.

Ms. Woo: Milad has asked an excellent question about gas.

Narrator 2: Milad smiled broadly and gave a mock bow to the class.

Ms. Woo: I think we're ready to do an observation. I'll be bringing a plastic bowl to each table. Each of you needs to write a description of what is in the bowl. What are the elements of a good description?

Magda: How it looks and if it makes any noise.

Hunter: What it feels like.

Milad: How it smells and how it tastes!

Ms. Woo: We're just going to use four senses today. No one should be tasting what's in the bowls.

Milad: Awww . . .

Narrator 1: Milad, Hunter, and Magda stared at the flat, white substance in their bowl.

Magda: It looks kind of like sour cream. Wet and shiny on top.

Hunter: No, it's more like whipping cream. It must be runnier than sour cream.

Narrator 2: Milad reached out and touched what was in the bowl with his finger.

Milad: That's funny. It looks like a liquid, but it feels kind of smooth.

Narrator 1: Magda and Hunter put their fingers in the bowl. Milad tried to grab a handful of the white liquid.

Milad: Look! I can make it into a ball!

Hunter: No you can't. It's melting right in your hand.

Magda: Maybe Milad just has really hot hands.

Hunter: Or the melting point is super low.

Milad: This is so neat!

Narrator 2: He squeezed another handful of the white substance. He pretended to throw it at Magda.

Magda: Stop that! Oh, look, you got some on my shirt.

Ms. Woo: Milad, throwing is not one of the five senses. Magda, calm down. In a minute the spot will dry and you can just brush it off.

Narrator 1: Hunter dipped his finger in the bowl and cautiously sniffed the white substance. It dripped back into the bowl like white glue.

Hunter: It doesn't have much of a smell.

Magda: It smells sort of powdery.

Milad: Powder isn't a smell!

Ms. Woo: In a minute you'll need to wipe your hands off and start writing your observations.

Hunter: Looks like a liquid, kind of holds a shape like a solid.

Magda: Does it stay solid longer if it's not in your hand?

Narrator 2: She dropped a ball of the substance on a paper towel and kept another of the same size in her hand.

Milad: Doesn't exactly feel dry, doesn't exactly feel wet.

Narrator 1: Milad made a fist and smacked it down into the bowl. Hunter and Magda jumped back.

Magda: Milad! You're going to splash it all over!

Narrator 2: Milad's hand hit the substance, but it all stayed in the bowl.

Hunter: It does make a sound when you hit it. Do it again, Milad.

Ms. Woo: Everyone needs to start writing starting now. Don't worry about getting your hands clean. Everything will dry and flake off. Just wipe off the big chunks.

Narrator 1: Milad whispered to Hunter and Magda.

Milad: My description is going to be way better than yours!

Hunter: You wish!

Magda: How come?

Milad: Because I know how it tastes!

Magda: You're not supposed to eat it!

Milad: I couldn't help it. When I smacked my fist down, a tiny bit flew into my mouth.

Hunter: I'm pretty sure good scientists do experiments with their mouths shut.

Magda: Yeah, or they died early in their careers.

Milad: You're just jealous. The school wouldn't let us experiment with something poisonous.

Hunter: Just you wait. Maybe after lunch you'll find out if this stuff shows up in the third state of matter.

Narrator 2: Milad made a face and looked up at the clock. It was almost lunchtime.

Narrator 1: Hunter, Milad, and Magda began to write.

The Way Things Work in Miniature

by Chris Gustafson
NSES 2, Evidence, Models, Explanation

Vocabulary Activity

On the vocabulary page, students will draw a cartoon illustrating the meaning of each of the vocabulary words.

Vocabulary Words

condenses—water vapor turns into water

evaporation—the process by which water is converted to a gas

model—a small representation of something else

terrarium—an enclosed container for observing plants indoors

Before Reading

Make an overhead of the graphic organizer and work as a class to name a type of model and list all parts of the model they can think of in the middle column, then the parts of those parts in the third column. For example, in a model of a car, car would be in the first column, interior and exterior in the second column, seats, steering wheel, dashboard in the third column opposite interior, etc. Or have students do this activity individually or in groups.

Perform *The Way Things Work in Miniature*

Cast of Characters

> Narrator 1
> Narrator 2
> Mr. Washington—*well organized, keeps things rolling*
> Rosa—*pragmatic, a bit impatient*
> Chamika—*a perfectionist, cares about appearances*

After Reading

What are the elements of a good scientific model? Ask students to brainstorm them, then give students one class period to create a scientific model from one piece of tagboard, scissors, staples, tape, and marking pens. Evaluate by having a gallery walk of the models or have each student briefly describe the model for the class.

Education Development Center, Inc. *Changes of State: An Elementary Insights Hands-On Inquiry Science Curriculum,* 1994.

The Way Things Work in Miniature Vocabulary

Draw a cartoon in each of the boxes below to illustrate the vocabulary words.

terrarium	**evaporation**
model	**condenses**

Name _____ Period _____ Date _____

Graphic Organizer

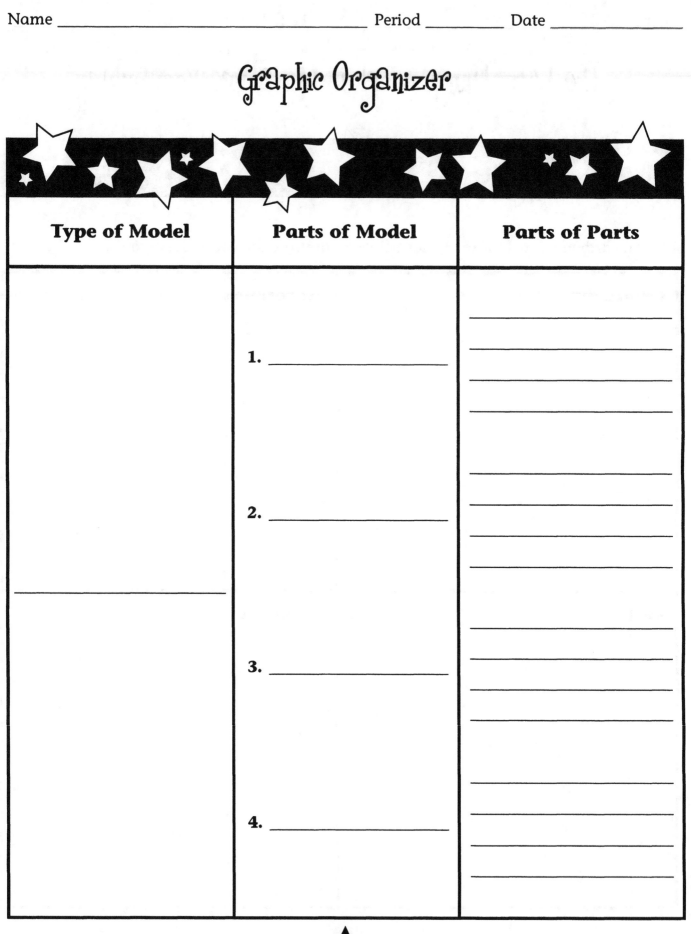

Type of Model	Parts of Model	Parts of Parts
_____	1. _____ 2. _____ 3. _____ 4. _____	_____ _____ _____ _____ _____ _____ _____ _____ _____ _____ _____ _____ _____ _____ _____ _____ _____ _____

The Way Things Work in Miniature

by Chris Gustafson

NSES 2, Evidence, Models, Explanation

Mr. Washington: All the materials are out on the counter for your final project. This is your chance to show what you've learned about states of matter. You'll create an environment in a terrarium that will keep plants healthy and growing.

Narrator 1: Rosa measured out some soil, chose a plastic bottle, and picked up a small foil tray. She carried it all back to her table.

Rosa: Chamika, just grab us some plants. You don't have to look at every one.

Narrator 2: Her partner Chamika carefully lifted up a tiny plant. She held it up close and examined the leaves. Then she set it back on the counter a little apart from the others, walked away, turned around, and squinted at the plant.

Rosa: Chamika, this is not the swimsuit competition in the plant beauty contest. Just pick one that looks healthy and get over here.

Chamika: They all look healthy. Except maybe that one, with three brown leaves.

Rosa: So it doesn't matter which one.

Chamika: It matters to me. I want our terrarium to be the most beautiful.

Narrator 1: Chamika chose the plant she had set aside from the others. By the time she picked the second plant, Rosa had crossed Chamika's name off of the experiment log they were supposed to keep together.

Narrator 2: Chamika pointed to the paper.

Chamika: What's that about?

Rosa: If you're not going to help, you're not going to get credit.

Chamika: Oh, get over it Rosa. Everyone else is cutting the top off his or her bottle. We better get going.

Rosa: Uh, that's what I've been telling you!

Mr. Washington: Most of you have your bottles cut and the soil spread in the bottom.

Narrator 1: Rosa struggled to get her scissors through the plastic. The blade slipped and gouged her thumb.

Rosa: Oww! It's all your fault! If you hadn't been so pokey, I wouldn't have to hurry now.

Chamika: Let me get a Kleenex. Here, I'll finish cutting this. You do that direct-pressure-to-the-wound thing. Relax, Rosa.

Narrator 2: Chamika spread the soil in the bottom of the bottle. She smoothed it evenly. Then she picked up the first plant, grabbed it around the stem, and carefully pulled it out of the pot.

Narrator 1: A pot-sized clump of dirt came out with the plant.

Rosa: Squeeze the dirt so the roots get used to growing out of the pot.

Chamika: I am, I am. Yes, you beautiful plant. You are going to grow big and strong in our terrarium!

Rosa: I don't think science has ever proved that talking to plants does any good. Just get it planted.

Chamika: How's your thumb.

Narrator 2: Rosa pulled aside the Kleenex. The bleeding had almost stopped.

Chamika: Mr. Washington, Rosa needs a band-aid.

Mr. Washington: Here you go, Rosa. Wash that thumb off before you put the band-aid on.

Narrator 1: Rosa finished the first aid on her thumb. Then she picked up the foil pan.

Chamika: It goes right here, and I'll put the plant on the other side. No, don't just set it on the dirt. Dig it down so it's level.

Rosa: Why? It's just there for evaporation.

Chamika: This way it looks like a little pond.

Rosa: It's just a science model! It's not like we're going to live there and swim in the pond.

Chamika: That's why it has to look good. Because it's a model. It's supposed to be an example of how things really work. I want things to look good and work right.

Narrator 2: Chamika rummaged around in her pencil pouch. She pulled out two tiny paper ducks.

Narrator 1: Each duck was glued on to the end of a toothpick.

Rosa: Do you know what's going to happen in our terrarium?

Chamika: Sure. The plants, the little pond. It all works together and water condenses and it keeps the plants alive.

Rosa: So what do you think will become of your paper ducks? They'll melt for sure.

Chamika: I don't think so. I put three coats of clear nail polish on them.

Narrator 2: Chamika pushed the toothpicks down into the dirt. One duck stood at the edge of the pond, looking ready to jump in. The other duck waited under the taller plant.

Mr. Washington: Groups, you should be just about finished. Make sure your ponds are full of water, and then rubberband the plastic wrap on the top of your terrarium.

Chamika: I know just where we should put ours. On top of the heat vent over by the window.

Rosa: Well, okay. I guess it does look pretty good. Why do you want to put it there?

Chamika: More heat will make more moisture.

Narrator 1: Chamika pulled out a piece of masking tape and a
silver jelly roller pen. She wrote her name on it with a flourish.

Narrator 2: Then she looked at Rosa, and very deliberately printed Rosa's name next
to hers.

Rosa: Oh, all right. You really did make our terrarium look better.

Narrator 1: Rosa pulled out the experiment log.

Narrator 2: She wrote Chamika's name above the place where she had crossed it out.

Melting an Ice Cube

by Chris Gustafson

NSES 3, Constancy, Change, Measurement

Vocabulary Activity

Students will work individually or in groups to fill out the example/description/comparison chart of vocabulary words for this selection

Vocabulary Words

container—something that holds other objects

data collection—recording what you measure or observe

graph—a diagram representing mathematical data

indented—pushed in

insulation—material to keep heat in or out

pistachio—a kind of nut

shredded—pulled apart into small pieces

Before Reading

In pairs, have students list all the ways they can think of to melt an ice cube. Share ideas with the class.

Perform *Melting an Ice Cube*

Cast of Characters

Narrator 1

Narrator 2

Ms. Juarez—a pack rat

Rodrick—well prepared

Thomas—kind of a flake

After Reading

Have students work individually or in pairs to list at least ten items, their current state, and a way the state of each item could be changed. Create an all-class list.

Education Development Center, Inc. *Changes of State: An Elementary Insights Hands-On Inquiry Science Curriculum,* 1994.

Name _____ Period _____ Date _____

Melting an Ice Cube Vocabulary

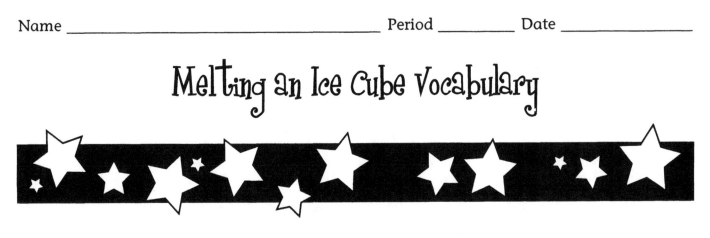

Fill in each box. Give an example of, description of, and comparison for each word.

	Example	Description	Comparison
insulation	A down comforter	Something wrapped around an object to keep it hot or cold.	Insulation is to a coffee cup as fur is to a cat.
container			
pistachios			
data collection			
graph			
indented			
shredded			

75

Melting an Ice Cube

by Chris Gustafson
NSES 3, Constancy, Change, Measurement

Narrator 1: The counter at the back of the science room was thinly covered with what could have been outtakes from the teacher's recycling bin.

Narrator 2: Ms. Juarez picked up some of the things on the table, showing them off like she was on the Home Shopping Channel.

Ms. Juarez: Here's some lovely shredded newspaper. And packing peanuts! There's a little bit of bubble wrap left. But mostly this experiment will rely on what you brought from home. Who remembers what you were supposed to bring. Rodrick?

Rodrick: Insulation. Anything that might keep something warm.

Ms. Juarez: That's right. Today you and your partner are going to design an insulated container for an ice cube. You'll have twenty minutes to build your container. Then everyone will get an ice cube and we'll keep track of the time it takes for each one to melt. Go ahead and get started.

Narrator 1: Roderick turned to his partner, Thomas. He pulled a sack out of his backpack.

Narrator 2: Roderick emptied his sack on the desk.

Thomas: Wow, you brought a lot of stuff!

Roderick: Cotton puffs, and a cereal box, and some sawdust from my Grandpa's workshop.

Thomas: And one of those plastic boxes for when you take soap on vacation.

Roderick: I thought we'd put the ice cube in that and pack all this other stuff around it.

Ms. Juarez: Remember that you'll have to be able to take the top off your insulated container every five minutes to check on your ice cube, so don't pack everything too tightly.

Thomas: What's this for?

Roderick: My Dad puts foil over the fried chicken to keep it warm after it's cooked. So I thought maybe it could keep heat out too. What did you bring?

Narrator 1: Thomas reached into his backpack.

Narrator 2: He poked a few things around at the bottom.

Thomas: Well, I actually forgot. But I brought some pistachios in this a couple of days ago, and it's not too gross.

Narrator 1: Thomas handed Roderick a plastic margarine container.

Roderick: You forgot? Thanks a lot! Why'd I have to get you for a partner?

Narrator 2: Thomas took the lid off the container and poured out a couple of pistachio shells.

Thomas: It's pretty clean. What if we put the ice cube in that traveling soap thing and packed something around it, and then put it in this margarine thing and packed it in more stuff?

Roderick: I guess it's worth a try.

Ms. Juarez: I'll be handing out the ice cube to each group in five minutes.

Thomas: Let's put some of the sawdust in the soap thing and make a kind of nest for the ice cube.

Roderick: Then we could put that in the margarine tub and stuff cotton puffs around it.

Thomas: Could we still get the lid off to check the melting?

Roderick: Sure. I guess we won't need the cereal box. Let's just crumble the foil around everything.

Ms. Juarez: Okay, when I come around to each group, show me where I should put the ice cube. I'll be moving quickly so everyone will get their ice cube at about the same time.

Narrator 1: Roderick pointed to the indented spot in the sawdust. Ms. Juarez gently set the ice cube in it.

Narrator 2: Thomas crammed the lid on the soapbox. They finished packing it in the margarine tub.

Roderick: It will be easy to take out the cotton puffs when it's time to check.

Ms. Juarez: While we're timing the melting, everyone needs to get out a piece of paper for data collection. We'll be graphing what you find out.

Narrator 1: When it was time to graph the data, Thomas and Roderick's ice cube didn't melt first, and it didn't melt last. It was right in the middle of the melting times.

Roderick: Not bad results. I guess we had plenty of insulation. We didn't even need my cereal box.

Thomas: No hard feelings?

Roderick: Naw.

Narrator 2: Thomas grinned, dug into his pocket, and handed Roderick a pistachio.

Hoping for a Thermal Transfer

by Chris Gustafson
NSES 4, Evolution and Equilibrium

Vocabulary Activity

List the vocabulary words on an overhead, the board, or a poster. Individually or in pairs, have students create an analogy statement for each of the words, for example "sulky is to unhappiness as cheerful is to happiness."

Vocabulary Words

Pistachio—a type of nut
sulky—unhappy, reluctant
therma—having to do with heat

Before Reading

As a class, in groups, or individually, use the Venn Diagram to compare heat and cold, keeping their individual characteristics in the separate circles, and the characteristics they have in common in the overlapping area.

Perform *Hoping for a Thermal Transfer*

Cast of Characters

Narrator 1
Narrator 2
Mr. Cado—enthusiastic, a bit nervous
Rachel—conscientious
Emily—spacey, boy-obsessed

After Reading

Assign half of the students to complete a character profile sheet on Emily, the other half on Rachel. Pair students who have done different characters to use their character profiles to create a comparison chart on the two characters.

Education Development Center, Inc. *Changes of State: An Elementary Insights Hands-On Inquiry Science Curriculum*, 1994.

81

Name _____ Period _____ Date _____

Before Reading Activity: Venn Diagram

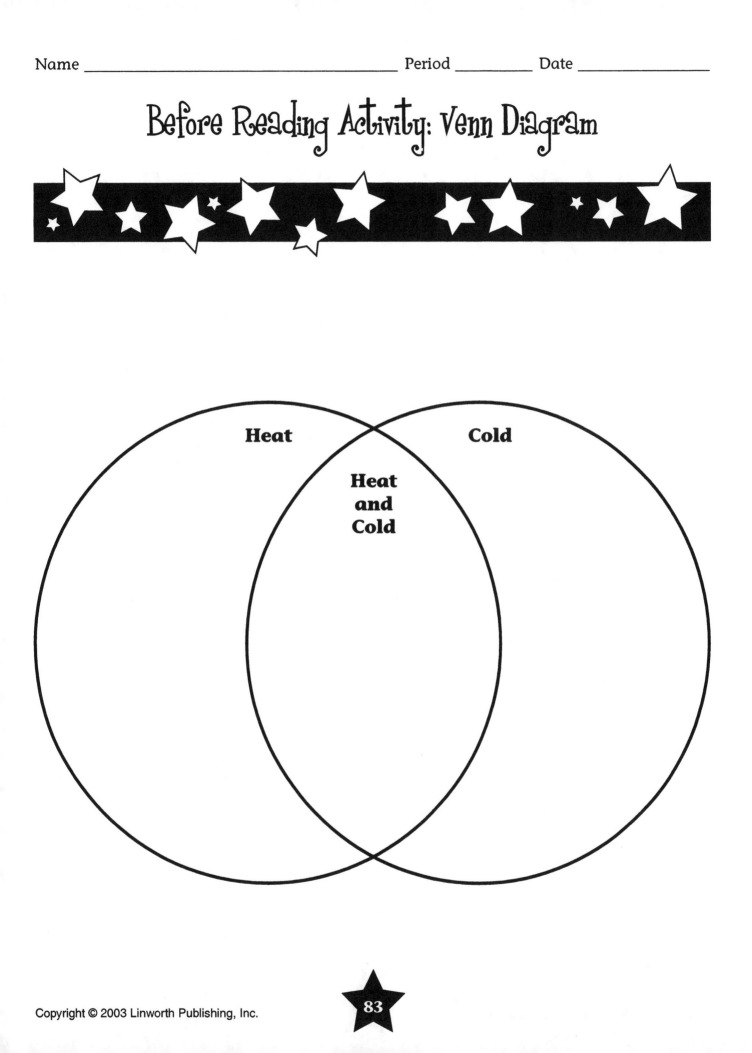

Heat

Cold

Heat and Cold

Hoping for a Thermal Transfer

by Chris Gustafson
NSES 4, Evolution and Equilibrium

Narrator 1: The science class was divided into pairs. Their job was to brainstorm ideas for an experiment.

Narrator 2: Mr. Cado, their enthusiastic student teacher, explained the assignment.

Mr. Cado: Okay, energy transfer. What do you know about it? How does it work?

Narrator 1: There was a long silence. Mr. Cado sighed.

Mr. Cado: Let's try again. What happens when something hot gets next to something cold?

Narrator 2: Rachel raised her hand. Mr. Cado looked incredibly relieved.

Mr. Cado: Rachel?

Rachel: The heat energy, what's it called?

Mr. Cado: Thermal energy.

Rachel: Right, that flows from the warmer to the cooler thing. They end up the same temperature after a while.

Mr. Cado: Exactly! Now, in your pairs, I want you to brainstorm experiments that would demonstrate what Rachel said about energy transfer. You have five minutes.

Narrator 1: Rachel turned to Emily, who was sitting next to her.

Narrator 2: Rachel pulled out a piece of notebook paper and a mechanical pencil. Emily picked at her nail polish.

Rachel: Any ideas?

Emily: Yeah, I think I need to put two top coats of polish on next time. This chipped really badly.

Rachel: Umm, that would be thoughts about heat transfer. Like when my cat comes in from outside in the winter, the pads on his paws are really cold. I wonder how long it takes him to walk around before his feet are room temperature again? That would be kind of hard to measure.

Emily: We have to write something down.

Rachel: Well, okay. Is there anything you wonder about? Mr. Cado says that's where to start when you're designing an experiment.

Narrator 1: Emily smiled.

Emily: Well, there is something . . .

Narrator 2: Rachel picked up her pencil.

Rachel: What?

Emily: About James.

Rachel: James?

Emily: Do you think he likes me?

Narrator 1: Rachel looked across the room at James. She had never actually noticed him before. All she could see was the back of an orange tee shirt and a head of curly, brown hair.

Narrator 2: Emily stared at James dreamily.

Emily: We could do an experiment.

Narrator 1: Rachel gripped her pencil more tightly and pulled the paper closer.

Emily: If he looks over at me in the next minute, it means he likes me.

Narrator 2: Rachel put the pencil down.

Rachel: Well, it could mean that he needs to know what time it is. You're sitting right under the clock. Come on Emily, we don't have much time left.

Narrator 1: Emily's voice was sulky.

Emily: I already gave you my idea! We each did one so we're even.

Mr. Cado: Two more minutes, class.

Rachel: Whatever. We could freeze something, put it in a glass of water, and then see how long it takes until they are both the same temperature.

Emily: Like an ice cube?

Rachel: Well, no. Once the ice cube melted, it would be gone, so you couldn't measure its temperature.

Emily: I don't see why that's important. It would all be the same temperature like you said.

Rachel: No, it should be something that won't melt, like, I don't know, a marble or . . .

Mr. Cado: One minute.

Narrator 2: Rachel made a face.

Rachel: Come on, Emily. Help me out here!

Emily: Have you ever held hands with a boy?

Rachel: What?

Narrator 1: Emily gazed down at her chipped nails, and then back at James.

Emily: It's so romantic! When I was going out with Cory last winter, we'd be walking along, and my hand would be all cold, and then he'd grab it, and pretty soon it would be cozy and warm.

Narrator 2: Emily kept her eyes on James, but he didn't turn his head in her direction.

Rachel: Cold hands, warm hands. Emily, that's a great idea! Heat transfer!

Narrator 1: Rachel scribbled this last idea on her list.

Mr. Cado: Time's up!

Narrator 2: The class turned their attention back to Mr. Cado.

Emily: Rachel! He looked at me!

Character Sheet — Emily or Rachel (circle your character)

Age: _____

Likes:

_____

_____

_____

Dislikes:

_____

_____

_____

Hopes:

_____

_____

_____

Fears:

_____

_____

_____

Other:

_____

_____

_____

90

A Hot Dog!

by Chris Gustafson
NSES 5, Form and Function

Vocabulary Activity

The vocabulary page asks students to read new vocabulary words, and then analyze three words or phrases. Two of the words or phrases relate to the meaning of the vocabulary word; one does not. Students will cross out the word or phrase that does not relate, then write a brief explanation of why the remaining words go together.

Vocabulary Words

clustered—gathered
form—how something looks
function—purpose
muzzle—the nose of an animal
pulverized—smashed into small pieces

Before Reading

As a class, in groups or individually, make a form/function/critical characteristics chart. For example form = milk carton, function = hold liquid, critical characteristics = can be closed, holds liquid. List as many examples as possible.

Perform *A Hot Dog!*

Cast of Characters

> *Narrator 1*
> *Narrator 2*
> *Ms. Blanchard—creative, dog-loving*
> *Irina—fun-loving*
> *Michelle—likes to tease*

After Reading

Have students draw a design for a form that cannot possibly fulfill its function—a comb with no teeth, a pitcher with no opening for pouring, etc. Then have them draw a design for a form that would function better than existing forms for the same purpose.

Education Development Center, Inc. *Changes of State: An Elementary Insights Hands-On Inquiry Science Curriculum,* 1994.

A Hot Dog! Vocabulary

Two of the words or phrases relate to the meaning of the vocabulary word; one does not.
Cross out the word or phrase that does not relate, then write a brief explanation of why the
remaining words go together.

1. **form**   appearance   taste   shape

_____

2. **saliva**   touch   mouth   digestion

_____

3. **muzzle**   nose   a dog   tree bark

_____

4. **clustered**   near   apples   next to

_____

5. **function**   what it does   toads   catching flies

_____

A Hot Dog!

by Chris Gustafson
NSES 5, Form and Function

Narrator 1: The science class clustered around a table Ms. Blanchard had moved out onto the lawn in front of the school.

Mr. Blanchard: Come closer, everyone, so I don't have to shout. Today you're going to be solving a problem that has to do with form and function. Who remembers what that means?

Irina: Form is how something looks.

Narrator 2: Irina's friend Michelle called out.

Michelle: You're looking good, girl.

Irina: Hush up, Michelle.

Mr. Blanchard: That's a good start on form, Irina. But it's not just how something looks. Remember that Mystery Matter that looked like a liquid but acted a bit like a solid?

Michelle: Okay, so if it looks like a solid, it really has to be a solid.

Mr. Blanchard: Right. That's its form. How about function?

Narrator 1: No one else raised his or her hand, so Irina blurted out.

Irina: That's what it does. Like Michelle's function is to give me the potato chips out of her lunch every day.

Michelle: You wish! That's being a friend, not being a function.

Narrator 2: A car pulled into the parking lot. A woman in sunglasses got out of the car and opened the back door.

Narrator 1: Out jumped a huge golden lab. The woman snapped a leash on the dog's collar.

Narrator 2: The dog panted and pulled on the leash.

Mr. Blanchard: All right! I was worried we'd have to do this activity without Dagmar. Class, this is my wife Maura and our very thirsty dog, Dagmar.

Michelle: Cute!

Irina: I hope she doesn't drool. I hate it when dogs drool.

Narrator 1: Dagmar sat next to Maura. He kept panting.

Mr. Blanchard: One thirsty dog. Fifteen teams of you, each with a bowl of ice cubes. It turns out ice is the wrong form of water to fulfill the function of a drink for a hot dog. Your job is to turn your ice cubes into water as quickly as possible. You may use any strategy you can think of, but you may not go off school grounds or out of my sight.

Narrator 2: Mr. Blanchard pulled an ice chest from under the table, put two big scoops of them in each bowl, and handed a bowl to each team.

Irina: Michelle, what are we going to do?

Michelle: I don't know. Let's see what everyone else does. Look at Tim.

Narrator 1: Tim and his partner sat on the ground cross-legged with the bowl between them. They were blowing on the ice cubes.

Irina: I think that would work better if their heads weren't shading the bowl.

Michelle: There's no way that's going to melt before next Thursday. What's Leann doing?

Narrator 2: Leann had her hand on the hood of the car that had brought Maura and Dagmar. It must have still been warm from the engine, because she set her bowl of ice on it.

Narrator 1: Irina wandered over to Dagmar and began to scratch her behind the ears.

Irina: Hey good dog. Don't your drool on me. Ick!

Narrator 2: Drops of saliva dripped from Dagmar's mouth.

Irina: Think, Michelle. We've got to get this dog some water.

Michelle: We've been doing stuff with ice all week. Usually when teachers give you a project they want you to figure something out. What do we know about melting ice?

Irina: We just let it sit and melt. That took a long time. Then we tried to make it melt slower.

Michelle: That's not going to help.

Irina: I know! Who won the melting contest?

Michelle: That was Leann. But there wasn't any car motor to use.

Narrator 1: Irina reached down and picked up a marble-sized rock that had been kicked onto the lawn.

Irina: Ice cubes melt faster when they're smaller. Leann pulverized her ice cube with the handle of her eyelash curler.

Narrator 2: Irina and Michelle hunted down larger rocks. There was already a little water in the bottom of the bowl when they began to smash their ice cubes to pieces.

Michelle: Don't worry, Dagmar. We're fixing you a drink.

Narrator 1: Soon the plastic bowl was full of slush. Michelle and Irina rushed the bowl over to Dagmar. Tim was still panting and blowing on his bowl. Leann was slouching by Maura's car. No one else was close to having water.

Mr. Blanchard: There you go, Dagmar, girl. Drink up.

Narrator 2: Dagmar slurped down the slushy water. Then she wagged her tail and nuzzled Irina. Water dripped off Dagmar's muzzle and on to Irina's feet.

Irina: Ick! Drooling dog!

Michelle: She's not drooling. It's just the water we made for her.

Narrator 1: Michelle's forehead was beaded with sweat. Irina's face was flushed. Smashing ice cubes was hot work.

Irina: I'm thirsty. Does anyone have anything to drink?

Narrator 2: There was a little bit of melted ice in the bottom of Tim's bowl. He offered it to Irina.

Michelle: Don't drink it, Irina. He's been blowing on it! It's got guy germs.

Irina: Ick!

Narrator 1: But she reached for Tim's bowl and drank it down.

Printed in the USA
CPSIA information can be obtained
at www.ICGtesting.com
LVHW080723170724
785510LV00007B/273

9 781586 831516